D1060842

EXTREMELY *Weird* ANIMALS

ANGLERFISH

BY CHRISTINA LEAF

BELLWETHER MEDIA • MINNEAPOLIS, MN

Jump into the cockpit and take flight with Pilot books. Your journey will take you on high-energy adventures as you learn about all that is wild, weird, fascinating, and fun!

This edition first published in 2014 by Bellwether Media, Inc.

No part of this publication may be reproduced in whole or in part without written permission of the publisher. For information regarding permission, write to Bellwether Media, Inc., Attention: Permissions Department, 5357 Penn Avenue South, Minneapolis, MN 55419.

Library of Congress Cataloging-in-Publication Data

Leaf, Christina, author.
  Anglerfish / by Christina Leaf.
     pages cm. – (Pilot. Extremely Weird Animals)
  Summary: "Engaging images accompany information about anglerfish. The combination of high-interest subject matter and narrative text is intended for students in grades 3 through 7"– Provided by publisher.
  Audience: Ages 7-12.
  Includes bibliographical references and index.
  ISBN 978-1-62617-072-8 (hardcover : alk. paper)
  1. Anglerfishes–Juvenile literature. I. Title.
  QL637.9.L6L43 2014
  597.62–dc23
                          2013035937

Text copyright © 2014 by Bellwether Media, Inc. PILOT and associated logos are trademarks and/or registered trademarks of Bellwether Media, Inc. SCHOLASTIC, CHILDREN'S PRESS, and associated logos are trademarks and/or registered trademarks of Scholastic Inc.

Printed in the United States of America, North Mankato, MN.

TABLE OF CONTENTS

A LIGHT SNACK

A small fish swims near the bottom of the Atlantic Ocean, looking for food. There is no light down here by the ocean floor. Slowly, a tiny blueish green light emerges from the depths. The small fish thinks it has found its meal and swims toward it.

As the light gets brighter, it illuminates rows of sharp, pointed teeth. Behind these teeth waits the gaping mouth of a female anglerfish. Despite her light, this round fish has skin as dark as night that helps her blend in. The small fish has no idea it is in danger. It continues swimming toward the light. At the last second, the anglerfish's huge mouth opens even wider and then suddenly snaps shut over the small fish. The anglerfish has caught another meal.

CREATURES OF THE DEEP

Anglerfish are a diverse group of fish with many different families and species. More than 300 species have been discovered so far. They vary in looks depending on their species. However, all anglerfish are strange-looking creatures known for their huge heads and toothy, crescent-shaped mouths.

Anglerfish come in many different sizes. The females of some species can be as large as 3.3 feet (1 meter) long. Most are much smaller. They are usually a little less than 1 foot (30 centimeters) in length. Males tend to be much smaller than females. Many male anglerfish are less than 1 inch (2.5 centimeters) long. Despite their small size, males are better swimmers. Their small, narrow bodies allow them to glide through the water easily. Females must waggle back and forth to move. Their bodies are mostly round with flatter sides and smaller fins.

human

anglerfish

Anglerfish can be found lurking in deep ocean water around the world. Most prefer the dark depths of the Atlantic. An anglerfish's color hints at how far it lives below the ocean's surface. Those found deep in the ocean are darker shades of gray, black, and brown. Their coloring helps them stay hidden in the murky depths.

N
W   E
S

Atlantic
Ocean

Europe

Africa

Deep-sea anglerfish live up to a mile below the surface of the ocean in the bathypelagic zone. This area is also called the midnight zone because sunlight does not reach this far down. The creatures that live here exist in complete darkness.

CASTING A LINE

illicium

esca

Anglerfish earn their name from a long, thin fin ray called the illicium. This is only found on females. The illicium extends out from the anglerfish's back and over its head. At the tip of the ray is an esca, which dangles in front of the fish's face. Together, the illicium and esca act like a fishing rod. The anglerfish draws food to itself just like human anglers who cast their lines.

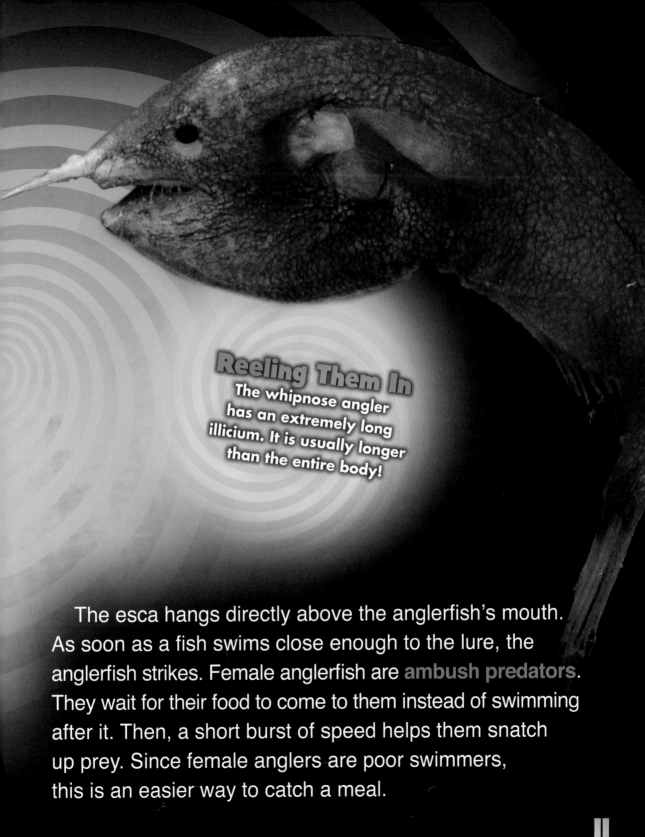

Reeling Them In

The whipnose angler has an extremely long illicium. It is usually longer than the entire body!

The esca hangs directly above the anglerfish's mouth. As soon as a fish swims close enough to the lure, the anglerfish strikes. Female anglerfish are **ambush predators**. They wait for their food to come to them instead of swimming after it. Then, a short burst of speed helps them snatch up prey. Since female anglers are poor swimmers, this is an easier way to catch a meal.

In the darkness of the ocean, it can be hard to attract prey. Deep-sea anglerfish make up for this with a glowing esca. The natural lure is lit by tiny **bioluminescent** bacteria. They give off a pale blue light that shines through the darkness of the water. Smaller fish swim toward the light thinking they have found a meal. They do not realize that they will soon become dinner for the anglerfish.

The bacteria live inside the anglerfish's esca their whole lives. Scientists are still not sure how the bacteria get into the lure. Some believe they sneak in through tiny holes in the skin. Others think anglerfish are born with the bacteria already inside of them.

Flashy Fish!
Some anglerfish
have other bioluminescent
parts that light up
their bodies.

Food is hard to come by in the deep ocean. The anglerfish does not know when its next meal will swim up. An anglerfish will not pass up a meal simply because it is smaller than its prey. It must snap at every opportunity that passes by. Its body has adapted so that it can eat almost any animal that comes its way.

The anglerfish's extremely large mouth can take up the bottom half of its face. The crescent shape of its mouth gives the anglerfish a constant frown and lets it open wide. The anglerfish can also **dislocate** its jaw. This allows it to open far wider than the normal bones and joints are able. The anglerfish also has thin, bendy bones. They help a dislocated jaw fit large prey.

Many deep-sea anglerfish can dislocate their jaws quickly enough to form suction. This pulls the prey closer without a fight. Some species of anglerfish also have retractable teeth. When an animal is sucked in, it can slide easily into an anglerfish's stomach without getting caught on sharp teeth. Then the teeth drop back down to trap the prey inside the fish.

As soon as an anglerfish swallows a large animal, its stomach immediately expands to fit the prey. It can stretch to fit animals twice as big as the anglerfish! The anglerfish digests this food very slowly. This means it can wait a long time in between meals without getting too hungry.

Anglerfish have names that sound as scary as they look. Many deep-sea anglers are in the seadevil family. Some species include the prickly seadevil, the warty seadevil, and the wolf-trap seadevil.

HITCHING A RIDE

Food is not the only thing that is hard to find in the depths of the ocean. It is also difficult to find other anglerfish in the dark. The female's lure is thought to help male anglerfish find her.

For most species of anglerfish, males are unable to survive alone in the dark for very long. They do not have the special traits that females have for hunting and eating. Instead, their goal is to find a female. They use a special smelling organ to find females in the dark. When a male locates a female, he bites her side with his sharp teeth and does not let go. Eventually, his body **fuses** to hers and he becomes a part of her. The male spends the rest of his life as a **parasite** of the female. Females can have more than one male attached to them. Some have as many as six on their body!

A Big
Difference
Females can be
60 times larger than
the males of the
same species!

STILL A MYSTERY

Much about the bottom of the ocean is still a mystery. There are many animals down there that have never been seen by human eyes. Sometimes, scientists just find one animal of a species, or only catch a glimpse on an **expedition**. This makes deep-sea creatures like anglerfish difficult to study. Without knowing more, it is hard to say how many anglerfish are still hiding in the deep.

There are some things we do know for sure, though. Temperatures in our oceans have been rising. Garbage and **pollution** are destroying the habitats of many ocean creatures. These problems will eventually affect the whole world. To keep learning about the mysteries of these bizarre creatures, we have to keep their homes safe and clean.

Anglerfish Fact File

Common Name: deep-sea anglerfish

Scientific Name: Lophiiformes

Nickname: seadevils

Famous Features: bioluminescent lure, expandable jaws
                        and stomach

Distribution: Atlantic Ocean

Habitat: ocean floor, often more than a mile
                        below the water's surface

Diet: fish, shrimp and other crustaceans

Life Span: unknown, but scientists
                        estimate 20 years
                        or more in the wild

Current Status: unknown

GLOSSARY

ambush predators—hunters that hide and wait for prey to come to them

bathypelagic zone—a part of the ocean about 3,000 to 13,000 feet (1,000 to 4,000 meters) below the surface; the bathypelagic zone is also called the midnight zone because sunlight does not reach it.

bioluminescent—organisms that create their own light

digests—breaks down food so that it can be used by the body

dislocate—to put a bone out of place

diverse—having distinct or unlike qualities

esca—the bait at the end of an anglerfish's illicium

expedition—a journey taken for a specific purpose

fuses—joins as if by melting together

gaping—wide open

illicium—a long, thin fin ray that extends from the back of an anglerfish

illuminates—brightens with light

parasite—an animal that lives by feeding off of another animal

pollution—harmful substances that affect an environment

retractable—able to pull back

suction—a sucking force created by drawing all the air out of a space

TO LEARN MORE

AT THE LIBRARY

Lunis, Natalie. *Glow-In-The-Dark Animals*. New York, N.Y.: Bearport Pub, 2011.

Lynette, Rachel. *Deep-sea Anglerfish and Other Fearsome Fish*. Chicago, Ill.: Raintree, 2012.

Owen, Ruth. *Anglerfish*. New York, N.Y. PowerKids Press, 2014.

ON THE WEB

Learning more about anglerfish is as easy as 1, 2, 3.

1. Go to www.factsurfer.com.

2. Enter "anglerfish" into the search box.

3. Click the "Surf" button and you will see a list of related Web sites.

With factsurfer.com, finding more information is just a click away.

INDEX

The images in this book are reproduced through the courtesy of: Minden Pictures/ SuperStock/ Masterfile, front cover, pp. 10-11, 18-19; David Shale/ Nature Picture Library, pp. 4-5, 9, 16-17; bierchen, p. 7; Bluegreen Pictures/ Alamy, pp. 12-13; Norbert Wu/ Getty Images, pp. 14-15, 18; Nature Picture Library/ SuperStock, p. 21.